MAYLEEN TORRES–HEW WING

Learned Lessons from My Busy Parent Life

How I'm Finding Peace and Balance in the Chaos

First edition

This book was professionally typeset on Reedsy.
Find out more at reedsy.com

To the little people in my life...
Ronin and Sohvay,
you have coloured my world and my life is full because you're in it.

To the big people in my life...
Sean,
for always choosing me and loving me no matter what

Mom & Dad,
for the unconditional love and support you've shown me throughout my life

I love you all <3

Contents

intro

If you're reading this, chances are you're a parent yourself. Now what was it that enticed you to pick up this book? Did you resonate with the "busy parent" part in the title? Or were you wondering how someone as busy as yourself can actually achieve peace and balance in what feels like a chaotic life? As inviting as that may sound, you have no idea where to begin feeling some sense of control in your life.

Let me tell you what I hope you will get out of reading this book but first, let me tell you what this book is not. It is not a book that will teach you about how to discipline your child or how to analyze your parenting style and be told of how you need to change it. There are plenty of books on that, those of which I've entertained reading and learning from and there are some real good ones out there that have helped me to understand my kids. These books have introduced me to strategies that have helped me along my parenting journey. So if that's what you were hoping for then I regret to tell you this is not that kind of book. However, if you stay the course, I hope you get some value by the time you finish this book.

While I appreciate when teachings in books tell you that their way is the guaranteed way to get results, I often take it with a grain of salt and make that decision for myself after I've tried out the suggested strategies and see how it works for me. And that's how I hope you approach this book. Take the lessons I've learned in my own busy parent life and see how it may apply in yours. I may offer very specific examples but I also will take a broader perspective and offer more principles to use. The most important thing is that you design the life you want and figure out what will work best for you.

I believe you can have anything you desire. There just has to be the right amount of motivation, drive, strong mindset, clarity, and action taking. That will be the secret to your success.

Now that must've thrown you for a loop. Why am I talking about success in a book about my busy parent life? Isn't that what we seek when choosing to read your typical parenting book? - How to raise successful children whether it's being top ranked in academics, sports or extracurricular activities, to raising socially responsible kids who want to save the environment. We read these books because we believe it's our duty as the guardians of our children to raise exceptional human beings and some of us may even get to the point of obsession. What do I mean by that? The second our child is born into this world, we have changed, we've transformed and morphed into a completely different person. We have become a parent who becomes consumed with our children. We are truly like butterflies. Once that caterpillar spreads its wings after it breaks out of its shell can it no longer go back to being a caterpillar again. A parent is just the same. We cannot go back to who we were before becoming a parent. Now our primary responsibility is focusing on raising our kids for at least the first 18 years of their life and even when they are grown and have their own lives we are, and always will be, bound to them because they are our flesh and blood.

In the rare times my husband and I actually have a child-free moment, like going out to eat at a fancy restaurant or a burger joint, it is almost guaranteed that one of us will say *"remember when we didn't have kids?"*. And that's all that needs to be said that brings us back to the days when we had so much more freedom to do what we wanted, when we wanted, without restrictions or having to take anyone else into consideration.

These days, before we can make plans for ourselves we have to figure out what we're going to do with the kids. Then we have to take into consideration more people into our plans - finding another set of responsible adults to watch my kids. *But I just wanted to go out for dinner... why does it feel like I'm an event planner for a wedding just to do this?*

In my single life (I use this term loosely to indicate the times I was not yet a parent) I just wouldn't have to think twice about it. All I needed to worry about was if I had shoes to go with my outfit.

So I digress, you get my point. The minute, no the second, we morph into the parent, some of us eventually feel like we lose a bit of ourselves. And so this book is first and foremost about us...we... me...the parent. This is a book that is intended to bring the focus back on ourselves.

Is this book about self-care (a big buzzword heard these days)? I guess to a certain degree, yes. But I do hope it's more than that; that the message isn't just about you taking a spa day for yourself. It's about finding yourself again if you feel like somewhere along the way you feel like you've lost who you are, or don't know who you are anymore (other than a parent to your kids). And there's this desire in you to feel whole again.

As one of my girlfriend mamas so eloquently put it...."*you gotta put one before two*". That's putting yourself above anyone else. Maybe one of the thoughts going through your mind is that I'm selfish for only thinking about myself or how dare I neglect my children and put my needs first? Okay, maybe that's a bit of an extreme interpretation but maybe some similar thoughts go through my mind when I've seen other parents thriving (not just surviving) and getting to do what they want and are living their best life and yet have kids of their own. Who's taking care of those kids? They must have a nanny. Well those judgmental assumptions and thoughts are probably nothing but me being jealous and just wanting that for myself. A life of balance, peace and happiness.

My hope is that in reading about the lessons I've learned through my personal experiences in this book, it will serve as a mirror to you and help you reflect on who you are and what it is that you truly want for yourself. And I hope that you will find a way to reach those desired goals because before we stepped into the role as a parent, we were an individual and we still are. Our point of view should be this - we are an individual, first and foremost, who is enhanced by the wonderful role of a parent among our many other roles. Our identity is not only that of a parent.

I AM (*insert your name here*). That's who you are. And your identity can be whoever you want to be. Let's not keep ourselves confined to a tick box on an application form (Single? Married? Number of Children?). We can be so much more. We just have to see it and believe it.

This book is not only intended to help uncover any blind spots for whomever reads this, it is just as much a means to help myself. Since I see myself as always a work in progress, I hope to continue to learn and grow alongside you.

chapter 1 - [The Chaos]

-Point A: Where I Stand-

The craziness I call my life does become overwhelming. I feel defeated because I feel I'm not productive with the things I need to and want to get done. It may not serve me to dwell on these feelings so much but it is just as important to be here than anywhere else. I've learned that before you can reach your destination (Point B) you have to know where your starting point is (Point A). Have you ever looked at a mall map? So you've found that shoe store on the map but wait, how do you get there? Which direction will you take? Well you have to find that sticker on the map that says "you are here". *Oh okay, so I have to go up to the next level, then make a right, pass the large department store, and after making the first left past the food court, I'll reach my destination.*

I remember one day standing in my kitchen making some homemade baby food for my youngest who was still under a year old while my eldest who was almost 4yrs old was running around in the house. I started having this unsettling feeling – I was feeling unhappy. But how is it that I could feel unhappy when having children should be a life filled with joy being in their presence? Well, that is both a true and untrue statement.

Yes, I love it when they make me laugh because they say and do the cutest things and come from a place of pure innocence. And they look at you with adoring eyes and give you unending hugs and kisses while being able to express *"I love you mommy"*. Now where is the dissatisfaction in that?

Oh yes, I remember now, it must be when I have to put these kiddos to bed and they just refuse to sleep and instead of hopping into bed and falling asleep peacefully like the angels I wish they could be, they're either playing with their toys or stalling to go to sleep asking for water because they're so thirsty and when I say no to any of these requests, the whining and crying just becomes unbearable. I can't forget to mention how suffocating it often feels when they are so heavily dependent on you where they're constantly seeking my attention 24-7 - especially when you're the milk supply and the human bidet.

The reality is that this is the typical parent life when your young kids are highly dependent on you. Thankfully, they eventually transition to becoming more independent and that's when you feel like you can breathe a little more.

But I take myself back to a moment where the feeling of unhappiness and despair came from a lack of feeling any sense of balance. And this was the moment when I realized how important balance was for me. When I felt like I was losing myself because all my time and energy was focused on the kids, I decided I needed to make some changes. But when I swung the pendulum too far the other way, all I felt was guilt for not making meaningful connections with them. I'd get caught up in checking my social media and spiral down the rabbit hole of viewing post after post after post with no end in sight.

My trigger was the damn tablet and tv. When it was bothering me how much they were on those electronic devices I knew I wasn't doing a great job being the parent I wanted to be for them - which was the parent who created memories with and for them. I could still hear my kid ask me *"mommy could you play with me?"* or *"mommy can we go outside?"* and you know what my response would be? *"Not right now, I'm doing something".* Well this something jumped from one thing to the next and the next thing you knew it was time to get them ready for bed. And often the things I'd be busy with would legitimately be the things that needed to get done around the house like washing the dishes, doing laundry, or paying some bills online.

-My Busy Life-

The busy life of a parent is inevitable. There is a shopping list of responsibilities that we are expected and obligated to do otherwise our household just can't function. When I think about my list it consists of:

- Going to work
- Managing the finances
- Putting food on the table
- Cleaning and organizing our living spaces
- Shopping for necessities
- Getting the kids ready for school
- Picking them up after school or daycare
- Taking them to their extracurricular activities or dentist appointments
- Helping kids with their school assignments and projects

- Supporting other family members (when parents get sick and need to be driven to a doctor's appointment)
- Attending social obligations (Thanksgiving, Easter, Christmas)
- Organizing events (kids' birthday parties, creating Halloween costumes and buying candies)
- Planning and taking that annual family trip
- Signing kids up for March break and summer camp

and somewhere I usually hope to squeeze in some time for myself (leisure interests, quiet me-time, time with friends, maybe a massage). I'm not sure that's an exhaustive list but as a parent yourself, you catch my drift. I'd say that's the typical life of a parent on a regular basis and then of course throw in a side of – *my car broke down now I have to get that fixed too* – and there's your recipe for a busy and chaotic life.

-Looking Forward to the Weekend?-

As I go through my work week, I put all my efforts, focus and energy into my 8 hr work day. Often I work through my lunch because the amount of work I have feels overwhelming and I don't want it piling up on me. Usually when I'm on a roll I don't let the clock stop me from working. Then when I think about the responsibilities I have when I'm at home, I don't have Fred Flintstone's work whistle blowing to tell me it's my lunch break; there's no time to sit on the couch and put my feet up on the ottoman and relax when I have so much to do.

This takes me to Friday - the end of my work week. A day most 9-5 employees look forward to. Once I arrive home after my hour-long commute, what I really want is to sit and relax but I don't because it's almost dinner time and we have to get food on the table. More often than not, however, cooking dinner on a Friday night when I'm so tired does not sound appealing so we take a survey - *"what food should we order for dinner tonight?"*. This actually is one of the hardest questions we have to answer in this house because our palates do not always enjoy the same thing. I have a son who is a foodie and can eat just about anything while my daughter on the other hand loves the typical kid acclaimed beige-meal-diet (pasta, bread, and cheese are her go-to's). My husband has a gluten insensitivity and I have no desire for any spicy food. So that typically leaves us opting for pizza, burgers and fries, Chinese food, or fried chicken.

On Friday nights, we've also adopted the family-movie-night tradition, that my kids very much look forward to, so we scroll through Netflix, Disney+ channel, or Prime to see what movie we've not already watched. You would think with the unlimited titles on these platforms that finding a movie should be easy but would you know it's actually pretty difficult to find a family movie that we all can watch that's appropriate for a 4 year old yet entertaining enough for an 8 year old? It's actually not easy at all so suffice it to say, we feel like we've watched all the movies available...and there's no way we'd watch a movie for a second time - that's sacrilege. And even though the movie may be entertaining enough for us all, it's not enough to keep myself or my husband awake because we're just so tired by the end of the week.

And so with popcorn bits and chip crumbs on the couch, the movie is over and we're dragging the kids to brush their teeth and getting them ready for bed, a task that probably takes another 30-45mins depending on how tired, cranky or wired these kids are. And of course with being tired ourselves, mommy and daddy have no energy to give these kids a bath so wipe-down it is! (If we even get to that point). Well, next thing you know it's now close to midnight.

-The Weekend Only Really Lasts 1 Day-

So, Friday is pretty much a write off now here comes the weekend baby! A Saturday morning could really go either way in our house. Ideally what I would want to happen is that I wake up as early as I would normally during the weekday while my kids sleep in, so I can either have a little time to myself or I can start getting some stuff done around the house. Let me tell you what actually happens...

I'm clearly too tired to get up after staying up late on a Friday night and because I do value some good sleep, guess who sleeps in and guess who wakes up at the sounds of the birds chirping before the sun rises? I have no idea how my kids can wake up earlier on the weekend than they do during a school day? In no way is it their circadian rhythm, it's them knowing that it's NOT a school day and they want to maximize the time on their devices. The rule we've been doing our best to follow is that they can only get their tablets beginning on Friday and there's no real limit that we've set on the weekends. We just have no energy or the time to police their tablet or tv usage because the reality is, Saturday is the only day I feel like I can get any housework done, and even then I don't feel like I do a great job accomplishing much.

Depending on the season and if I was able to catch some of the deadlines in time, I might have the kids enrolled in an extracurricular activity. As I write, I am proud to say I managed to get these kids signed up for gymnastics at the same time - now that's a win! But when they don't have an activity to go to, I barely get a chance to even take the kids outside for some fresh air or run around the park that we live right across the street from. Honestly, I don't know how other parents do it with their multiple kids and their rep teams or any activity at all. The irony of it all is that I grew up always involved in many extracurricular activities where my schedule was filled. What I knew I didn't want to do was stress myself out taking the kids to activities when I can barely get the essential things done around the house. However I know the benefits that it has for them so at most I would do my best to have the kids involved in at least 1 activity each. Once again...winning! I must admit that when we do a variety of different activities, I leave the weekend feeling like it was pretty full and eventful. But when we barely even leave the house and stay home, the weekend goes by extremely fast yet still wonder what the heck we even did.

Saturdays are also the day for classmates' birthday parties or visiting the grandparents. So no housework looks like it's getting done today. *It's a hang out kind of day but first, which of you kids want to come with me to buy your friend's birthday gift? On second thought, I renounce my invitation because these kids will only ask me to buy them something the second they step into the store.* As I turn the door knob and open the door I hear "Mommy, I want to come with you". "No! Mommy has to go now, just go back to your tablets". *Oh this is nice, time alone in the car is heaven for me. The peace and quiet – just me and my own thoughts.* Coming back home, it's almost dinner time and it's usually a toss up between ordering food (again) or getting myself in the kitchen.

Side note: I know it sounds like I'm the only parent involved and for the most part, yes, when it comes to the weekend because this is when my husband does most of his work. As a starting entrepreneur in the nutrition and cooking industry, this is his busiest time. During the week, he's responsible for grabbing the kids from school and preparing most of our meals which leaves me with the weekend shift. So, when do I fit in paying the bills? Laundry? De-cluttering and cleaning the house? Checking and answering some emails? I have no idea!

And then here comes Sunday poking its head reminding me that it's the day to start getting ready for a whole new week again.

Do the kids have enough school uniforms, underwear and cloth masks for the week? I'll run a load of laundry when I wake up and then I'll need to prepare their backpacks – oh no! I forgot to take their lunch bags out on Friday...eww gross, they didn't finish their fruit snacks and their thermos is smelly from their half eaten spaghetti!

What's this at the bottom of the bag? There's a school form that I have to fill out and it was due last Friday? How come I didn't see this and it was sent home last week?

Alright kids, time to get ready for bed – and of course after having no real routine over the weekend and having slept late on a Friday and Saturday night, it's a bit of a nightmare getting these kids to bed at a decent time that hopefully doesn't have them sleeping in the next morning. But we go through another week just like the one we had last and we relive it like a broken record.

chapter 2 - [Taking Inventory]

"How do I feel about my current situation?"

A broken record? So we go through the motions again? I stop and think, is this what life is all about? Just going through the motions of the day to day tasks just to get to the next day? These kinds of questions lead me down a path of deep inner self-reflection.

-The Feels-

I've learned to start my reflections with how I'm feeling. As I start here, simply put - dissatisfied. Maybe I shouldn't feel this way and just be grateful for all that I have because I know there are people in worse off situations than I am so I should have nothing to complain about. I am all for expressing my gratitude for all the blessings I have, however let me tell you why being "dissatisfied" is a good place to be. What it means to me is that I'm not going to be complacent and just take things as they are without wanting to aspire for more or better. I'm not going to be just a pawn in this game of chess and be swayed by the mundane of everyday life. I want more and it's okay to want that.

What exactly am I dissatisfied about? I'll be the first to say that when I'm feeling overwhelmed, stress takes over and it impacts all other areas of my life like the relationships I have: with my children, others and myself.

-Relationship With my Kids-

I know for a fact that when I'm stressed and overwhelmed I have very little patience which means I yell at my kids...A LOT! This comes out most at bedtime when I just want my kids to listen so that the night can end and once the kids are fast asleep I can get a few things done that I didn't get a chance to do after coming home from work. But they seem to think bedtime is synonymous with play time. My kids enter the world of WWE and think they're the Bushwhacker Brothers.

They're jumping on the bed, shooting nerf guns at each other, or re-enacting some marvel superhero movie. I try to keep my cool but to no avail - so I do what I normally do which is to yell at them to get their attention and it's somewhat effective but now I'm just irritated. I've even cried a few times because I'm also just exhausted and not only do I want them to sleep, I want to sleep too. Sometimes I yell so much that it puts my kids off and then gets them extremely upset at me. Then naturally I feel guilty for possibly overreacting and yelling at the littlest thing that triggered my yelling in the first place. I've listened to a good number of parenting audiobooks and let me tell you, when I'm triggered, there is no rational thinking or calm emotion coming from me. All those wonderful parenting strategies go out the window. I revert to ways of when I grew up being disciplined.

I know it seems like I have no control over my kids and yes, it often feels that way. So the only way I feel like I can get some sense of control is by yelling at them. This isn't the parent I want to be. I actually do want to have a strong bond and connection with my kids, especially at these young ages when they still want my attention and want to be around me. I know yelling at them and being irritated by everything they do is not the ideal path to achieving a strong bond. I'm acutely aware from many other parents that this time with them doesn't last forever. Since I am supposed to be a strong influence in their lives at these ages I don't want to mess them up. I just love these stages where I can witness their innocence, playfulness and creativity. I believe that if I don't focus on their needs while making sure they grow up with proper values and discipline, it may lead us down a path of bad behaviours and other unfavourable outcomes.

-Relationship with Others: My Hubby-

There are just as many other important relationships I have and want to foster beyond my kids. Before there were kids, there was a husband and a wife. While I'm grateful that my husband is now much more visible and present since quitting his 9-5 job at the bank, he and I are still quite disconnected. He's often in the zone doing his work from home while I tend to the kids or something household related. When we even try to have an adult conversation, our son's bionic ears radars in and will jump into our conversation and ask details about what we're talking about or will unknowingly interrupt our deep conversation wanting to ask his dad a video gaming question. Or my daughter will literally pull my arm to ask me to cook with her in her play kitchen or accompany her to the bathroom because she feels scared to be alone. Friends will tell me that we should schedule a date night. While this sounds fabulous, my husband and I just don't end up prioritizing us. Our work and family have usually come before all else. When we do have our date nights which can be counted on 1 finger - our anniversary - this once a year event is quite magical. It usually consists of dinner at a nice restaurant and adult conversation about...*what DO we talk about?* Reminiscing about the good 'ol days when we took vacations to Chicago, New Orleans, and San Francisco as a couple - sans kids. But of course we always find a way to circle back to talking about our kids somehow. Like I said earlier they are a part of us and forever will be. They cannot be erased from our conversations.

-Relationship with Others: My Parents-

Being an only child holds a great responsibility because there's no other sibling to fall back on when my parents need help with something. My husband has 2 older siblings who are able to help out with my in-laws when they need it so the load gets divided amongst them. It's challenging keeping a close relationship with my parents having 2 young children adding to the already busy life. If I can't even find the time to clean the bathroom sink, how do I find the time to make a meaningful connection with my parents? And when they're sick or need some technological help with their internet, computer or smart tv, who is it that they call on? Surprise! Surprise! It's me! Am I complaining? Not at all because I would want them to ask for help rather than have them struggle. The point I'm making is that they are going to call me because I'm the one they can rely on the most, however I'm only just 1 person with a few other responsibilities already going on. The demands will only increase as they age and I expect that. But fitting them in also means I neglect accomplishing other things in my life or just have to put them on hold. I want to be as available for them as I can be so I don't live life with any regrets when they're gone. Morbid thinking? Perhaps but I'm just being realistic. It brings my parents joy when they spend time with me and the kids so I do make an effort to make time for them. We didn't always have a close relationship when I was growing up but things have changed for the better so I want to ride that horse into the sunset. It brings me joy when they experience joy.

-Relationship with Others: My Friends-

I grew up cherishing my time with friends. Some of my fondest memories are of sleepovers at my BFF's home, running around outside in the concrete parking lot that served as our urban parkette. For us and the neighbourhood kids it was just as fun as, if not better than, the conventional park with swings down the street; or watching a crap load of tv from music videos on MuchMusic (Canadian version of MTV) to game shows and daytime soap operas. I am grateful that these friends, who are basically family, are still in my life. But these same friends also have busy lives with their kids. As much as our parents had busy work lives, they really valued their social connections with each other and as a result allowed us as kids to develop a strong bond with each other. I wish my kids were able to experience that and I admire (but secretly envy) people with big families who are close knit because their kids can grow up together with that same special bond. But I digress, I can't create an instant family out of my back pocket, however I am able to help foster those same bonds by making an effort to meet up with friends and their families. Easier said than done for sure because I know how hard it is to coordinate schedules with other people's schedules. This takes me to spending time with my own friends - without kids. I know first hand how difficult it is to find a time when 5 girlfriends can get together for brunch or dinner. Celebrating a friend's March birthday has now taken us into June! What is the point of all of this? A busy life makes it difficult to do all the things you want to do, especially when it comes to spending time with people other than your partner and extended family. Our friends tend to fall to the bottom of that hierarchy of people we want to spend time with.

-Relationship with Myself-

The thought of having a relationship with myself is how this book came to fruition. After reflecting on my busy life as a parent and how it has pulled me in directions I didn't even fathom before becoming a parent, I realize how much I value having balance in my life. It's when I feel in this state of balance do I feel this sense of true happiness. Because what this means to me is that my kids' needs are taken care of and my own needs are being fulfilled. What does it mean to have a relationship with myself? As much as I grew up a lover of music and attending as many concerts as I can possibly get to - I enjoy driving in my car listening to silence, not necessarily to the radio. I don't have very many moments of solitude where I'm not entertaining my kids' 10,000 questions or tending to someone's needs in the house. These are rare moments that I will jump at when there's an opportunity. So when there's an item at the grocery store that we need to have picked up, I won't hesitate to volunteer myself so I can have some of that peace and quiet. I am a lover of learning and reflecting so any opportunity I can get to listen to a podcast or audiobook, or any opportunity to write in my journal or jot down an insightful thought in my phone's notepad, that's what you might catch me doing.

Finally, with my health benefits from work, I wish I could say I take full advantage of the extensive massage therapy treatments I'm entitled to but this busy life of mine does make it difficult to squeeze that in somewhere unless I feel like it's really needed, and even then it warrants me having to take a day off from work for a little R&R.

These are just a few of the things that I wish I had the freedom to do without having to worry about how and when I will get to fit it in my schedule. But as I've learned in my journey, things are possible and I'm looking forward to sharing that in the upcoming sections of this book.

21

chapter 3 - [The Goals]

"What is it that I really want?"

-Point B: Where I Want to Be-

I recall a time in my career when work was consuming so much of my mental, physical and emotional energy that I didn't have any juice left for my family when I would get home. I was definitely in an unhappy and very unbalanced place. But I made some choices and changes that afforded me a better work-life balance that definitely led me to being in a much happier place. If there is one thing that I know for sure is that I don't ever want to have that same feeling again. But the feeling of an unbalanced life will creep up on me once and a while and that's when I have to re-evaluate my priorities so I can make adjustments and changes.

But before even getting to that point and before any action can be taken, what I need to get clear on is what I truly want and see for myself and my family. I've already alluded to some of those desires in the previous chapter where I focused a lot on relationships.

In truth, if there's one thing that I've always found challenging is finding clarity in what I want. Most of my subconscious programming has hindered my ability to see what is even possible in my life making it difficult to make that list of the things I desire, especially the things that may take time to accomplish or obtain.

There are great resources (like planners) out there that help people create and track their goals. Now, I will admit that being a goal setter isn't really my thing. I'm actually a "To-Do" Lister which is similar but on a smaller scale I suppose. I love my "Notes" app on my phone and it probably is one of the top 3 that I use on a regular basis. When any thought comes to my head, I jot it down there. But it is used the most every morning when I make that list of what I want to accomplish that day and for the week. Essentially, I focus on the tasks that are a priority for me; the non-negotiables of what has to get done. There's my "have-to-do" list for the week and then I have a separate "parking lot" list that I use for any other tasks that pop into my head but I know isn't something I'm going to prioritize for that week. Then I create my "daily-to-do" list that I pull from my master "have-to-do" list. Sounds complicated, I know, but what I want to point out is that this is what works for me. My "to-do" list paired with my commitment to complete the tasks equals accomplished tasks that I can place a check mark beside - and that's something I find most satisfying. If anyone knows me, I've always been a "Lister", to the point where I over-listed the things I needed to do - I would even list having to take my vitamins. I might as well have also listed "going to the bathroom" at the rate I was going. But of course, I had to find a way where I wasn't feeling overwhelmed by my own list because that had caused some anxiety at times thinking to myself how I would accomplish the tasks on my massive list.

If most people are like me and don't find goal setting an exciting task to do, I can absolutely relate to that. For one, if I create a goal and don't accomplish it, I don't want to experience the feeling of failure. Then I worry about how I'm going to even accomplish the goal with an already busy life. With these thoughts going through my mind, it doesn't make me feel very motivated to want to accomplish the goal so what's the point of even creating one to begin with? But what this is probably really telling me is that I've either created a goal that's too big or not important enough to me.

So to make goal setting a little more palatable I will share this exercise. While this may be easier for some but not for many, I hope you take this opportunity to follow along with me and just see where this leads. And remember there is no right or wrong answer with this; it's all about what's important and meaningful for you. No one has to even know what's on your list. If you don't like it, then you can scrap it and start again.

Let's give it a go!

Challenge #1: Take a moment to think about what you ideally want in each of these life areas (for you and/or your family). Fill out at least 3 points in each. Take into consideration what is a priority in each section.

RELATIONSHIPS

(How would you like to spend time with your Children, Partner, Family, Friends? What kind of relationship would you like to have with them?)

1.

2.

3.

CAREER

(What areas in your career do you want to focus on? What do you want to improve on or change? What do you want to learn about that will make your career more meaningful and enjoyable? Do you want or have a side business you want to start or grow?)

1.

2.

3.

LEISURE

(Where do you want to go on vacation? What are some fun events or activities you want to do for yourself and/or with your family? Are there any extra-curricular activities you want to enroll in for your family or yourself?)

1.

2.

3.

PHYSICAL

(Health, Fitness, Rest, Self-Care)

1.

2.

3.

HOME AND LIVING ENVIRONMENT

(Where do you want to live? – Location, Type of home; What does your home look like? – Clutter-free, organized, decorations; What other household projects/tasks do you need to or want to accomplish?)

1.

2.

3.

SPIRITUALITY/PERSONAL DEVELOPMENT

(Giving back to support community/charities; Journaling, Meditation, Learning)

1.

2.

3.

FINANCE

(Money goals that will afford you the things/experiences you would want or need to buy; items you want to purchase; Financial responsibilities – budgeting, investing, saving, taxes, planning)

1.

2.

3.

Challenge #2: Now, if you're up for a real challenge I implore you to entertain writing down 100 THINGS or MEMORIES you want to have and/or accomplish in 5 years (for yourself and your family). This will be your opportunity to think outside the box and think about the things that you believe may be even impossible to achieve. Write down items on your list as if money and time were no obstacle. Don't focus on how you will achieve these things, this is your opportunity to dream big. I would suggest using the same life areas/categories in Challenge #1 to help create your list.

chapter 4 - [Taking Action]

"So what? Now what?"

Well congratulations to us for getting to this point! Know that these are challenges I've also completed or am still currently in the process of doing. I think the hard part is out of the way which is determining what it is you really want. When you look at your list, does it feel overwhelming and insurmountable? Probably. But don't fret, this is where the magic starts to happen. What may feel unattainable will turn into what is possible because you will chip away at these goals a little bit each time. How does the adage go?...it's a marathon not a sprint (to the finish line – your goal).

Let me share how I approach a goal and make it manageable. The most important step after creating your goal is to break down the main goal into smaller tasks or action steps. If you are so inclined, you can create a timeline for the primary goal so that it may help guide you in how you want to create your smaller tasks. I could go into the details of creating a S.M.A.R.T. goal (Specific, Measurable, Attainable, Relevant, Timely) but I'm choosing not to because frankly that sometimes feels like too much pressure for me. I already tend to feel a lot of pressure from the busy life I already have so I'm choosing not to add the stress of a ticking timer counting down for me. However, for the goals that are extremely important for you to accomplish sooner rather than later, I think it's highly valuable to set a timeline or date you want to complete it by. A note to keep us all sane - we must give ourselves some grace if our goal isn't completed in the time we wanted. The most important thing to remember is that so long as we've set an intention and put forth some effort towards our goal, it's the progress towards the goal that should be celebrated; it's not always about the end result.

In addition to my daily and weekly "To-Do" list, I have a journal where I write down the 2 or 3 priorities I want to focus on for that day, keeping in mind how much time you have in your day so making sure that the priorities you set are realistic and attainable.

For each priority this is what it would look like:

1. I choose the category/area of my goal - Then indicate what's the primary goal
2. I write down the specific task I want to tackle that day towards the primary goal
3. I write down why this is important to me

Here's an example:

1. (Category) Relationship - (Goal) Spend time with Kids
2. (Specific task) Spend 30 minutes with the kids at the park
3. (Importance) I want to feel connected with my kids and give them some leisure/physical activity outside the house so they can be off their tablets

Why I feel it's valuable to do that last step and note down why the goal and task is important to me, it's what gives me the motivation to want to accomplish that task. We need something to give us the drive to take action with our task, so I do my best not to skip that part.

Finally, for a very important step, especially for someone like me who becomes easily distracted - I specifically write down 1 thing that I'm NOT going to do for that day. So to add to the above example:

· Today, <u>I WILL NOT</u> → Do any laundry

I find when I do these above steps, I am so much more productive in my day than when I don't do this at the beginning of my day. I also find that I accomplish more because I've gained momentum after accomplishing my prioritized tasks for the day. It's quite infectious checking items off my list so I either want to do more or I actually find I have the time to add in another task that I didn't expect I could do. This whole process allows me to be hyper-focused and committed to my goals.

chapter 5 - [The Tools]

"What has been working for me?"

-Keys To Having Balance and Peace-

So we've assessed how we're feeling and what our current situation is; then we created some goals we want to achieve; and we've just figured out the baby steps needed to reach our bigger goals. Is that all it takes to achieve that balance we want in our lives? In my opinion and experience thus far, I think there's a lot more to it. I've recently been on a journey of examining what makes someone successful. If I were to ask you to think about how you would define success, what does that mean to you? What do you think makes someone successful? What are the things that successful people do to manifest their level of success?

Maybe to some, success equates to wealth but for me it goes beyond that. I define success as working towards something that you love and are passionate about; with the constant efforts towards your goal, it is inevitable that you will arrive at your destination. I therefore consider ultimate success as achieving balance, happiness and peace in my life while doing what I love and fulfilling my family's needs and desires.

-Mindset-

Mindset it absolutely everything! If there's nothing else you take away from this book, know that to achieve anything you want in your life, it starts with how you think and what your beliefs are that contribute to your thoughts. Those conscious and subconscious thoughts that run through our mind every second have a lot of power over our behaviours and actions. Our mindset can either be beneficial or detrimental to us. If we're feeling stuck where we're unable to take proper action towards a goal, there's an opportunity to unpack and discover what is holding us back or blocking us - and I can guarantee it's a product of our mindset.

[Surrender, Let Go and Accept]: So, when my kids are unruly, my home is in disarray, or I'm late paying my bills I am learning to surrender, let go and accept what is. Or when there's a goal to work towards, I will just complete whatever task needs to be completed and tell myself *"I will do this one little thing and feel good about myself"*. Sometimes there is no point in getting so stressed over something because feeling or reacting to my stress doesn't change anything, instead I just have to have the mindset that something needs to change or be different.

[Perspective]: When there's a problem that surfaces and is beyond my control, I change my perspective from one where I place blame and fall victim to the circumstances to that of learning from the experience and see how the situation is actually serving in my favour. I don't let a situation defeat me but rather I always look for a solution to the problem; that is my way of taking responsibility and not playing the victim.

[Grace and Forgiveness]: When I feel like I haven't done a good enough job with something or accomplished what I set out, I give myself grace and forgiveness knowing that I've tried; but even if I didn't try hard enough, I know I can dust myself off and try again another time. Failing at something can actually be a blessing where it can be viewed as a great opportunity for learning and growth.

[Compassion and Understanding]: When my kids are an emotional wreck and it's triggering me to want to yell, I find peace through having compassion and understanding, knowing they are young and still have developing brains and emotions that are unlike an adult's ability to cope; yet also remembering that if I can react and get emotional as an adult, kids also have the permission to be their authentic selves by being fully expressed. Being vulnerable about my own feelings and thoughts helps keep me grounded and I avoid bottling up most of my pent up emotions that otherwise would explode if I didn't express myself in some form.

-Routine-

I'm the first person to admit that I have an aversion to routines because I just don't believe life will always unfold the way you expect. It becomes frustrating for me when I don't meet those timelines and because I put so much pressure on myself to get things done, I become very impatient and stressed out - the very opposite of what I'm wanting to feel. Sure, I want my kids to go to bed at 7:30 pm every night but life happens and in our household it doesn't always operate on a tight schedule like a well-oiled machine - we tend to have a few cogs out of place most of the time. Kudos to all those families who can manage a tight routine. However, that doesn't mean there's no value in having routines because

I wish I was better at following them myself.

When I challenged myself to do a morning journaling routine for 30 days, it was a game changer. I learned that I can actually commit to something that didn't seem possible at first. So for myself, I've been committed to waking up extra early in the morning before the kids wake up (around 5:30 am) and I do the following:

[Meditate]: good for rewiring my brain and body to remain calm in the chaos and to clear my thoughts.

[Journal]: to reflect on or dump any thoughts and emotions I'm feeling as a form of mental and emotional release.

[Gratitude]: reflecting on what I'm grateful for puts me in a high level of vibration allowing me to approach my day with a positive attitude and attract positive things throughout my day.

[Affirmations]: by declaring my affirmations it helps me focus on how I'm going to show up for that day and who I'm choosing to be to make it as successful a day as possible.

[Visualize and Manifest]: visualizing the goals I want to manifest allows me to embody the feeling I want to have when I envision already achieving my goal; this leads me to taking action towards my desired goal.

[To-Do List]: making my to-do list for the day helps keep me focused and productive

[Exercise/Physical Activity]: squeezing in a bit of exercise changes my physical state and raises my energy to have a good start to my day and contributes to any health/fitness goals I might have.

Sounds daunting, I know. However, I do these in a way that works for me. So long as some time is dedicated to each of these items in my morning routine or at some point throughout my day, even if it's a 5 minute meditation, 5 minutes of journaling, and 5 minutes of push ups, by putting forth some kind of effort, I consider that accomplishing my task. I have learned that creating a set of routine habits are one of the keys to success.

[Rest]: Finally, there is nothing more precious than sleep and rest. It offers the benefits of having optimal mental health, mood and physical health, increased concentration and memory, and reduced stress. I know I'm particularly cranky when I'm feeling tired which again leads to my impatience with my kids.

-Learning-

Having an open mind is an asset. Although we have every bit of information conceivable literally in the palm of our hands, we still can't know everything but we can have access to anything. We live in The Information Age and I think we are so fortunate to be able to learn anything we want in an instant. I'm a lover of learning and through the information I consume it helps me reflect on my own life and how I can make it better. We can learn and open up our minds by indulging in e-books, audiobooks, youtube videos, social media, podcasts, and articles or blogs on the internet. Long gone are the days where we walk down the street to our local library to pick up a tangible book - these days we don't have to leave our homes anymore to soak up all of this information.

From books to educational or personal/professional development courses, there may be redundancy with the information we consume but as I've learned through Bob Proctor's wisdom, in order to truly understand the concepts we've learned about, repetition is important. If ever you've said the words "I already know that so I don't need to learn that again" I may find a healthy debate in that statement. If there's one thing that I believe is that we are meant to grow, evolve and change but we have to choose this path. Being open to learning can only serve us for the better. And learning doesn't just happen through other people's opinions and writings, we must also be open to learning from our own personal experiences and not see it as something that is intended to defeat us or wear us down but it's there to help us grow wiser. I love the saying the rings so true...*"Life doesn't happen to you, it happens for you"* – Tony Robbins

If there is another piece of advice that I hope to pass along is to invest in yourself, in your personal development. Take a course, even if it's just 1, heck, if you're feeling adventurous, take 2! I have no regrets taking the courses that I have and the money I've spent on them because it has really allowed me to take that inventory of myself. It was an opportunity to look in the mirror and really examine who I currently am and transform into who I want to become. Had it not been for the personal development courses that started me on my path of growth, you probably wouldn't be reading the words on this page right now. It has really helped to shape my mindset first and foremost. Ponder on this: If you knew that what separated you from a successful person you admired was your mindset, would you look for ways of changing yours? If the answer is yes, go ahead and give yourself the gift of taking a course or working with a professional or coach.

-Seeking Help/Support-

As much as some of us may want to believe that we don't need anyone's help or support to thrive and achieve success, I would have to debunk that theory and bluntly say "you're wrong". We need as much support as we can get whether it's from family, friends, professionals or other support circles. While I enjoy expressing myself through writing with a pen on a piece of paper, nothing really compares to interacting and talking to another person. It's our chance to bounce ideas off of one another, to be able to see another perspective, or just have someone's ear to be your sounding board.

When speaking with a professional like a therapist, counselor, or life coach, their objective point of view can help guide you in the right direction, see where you're stuck and help you find the answers that are already within you; but often we get in our own way and just can't see the blocks for ourselves.

I've also learned that when aspiring for success, you want to be sur-rounded by like-minded people because "Proximity is Power" according to Tony Robbins. By surrounding yourself with people whom you want to emulate, you are inspired and motivated to become like them.

Lastly, when I reflect back during the days when I had a newborn, a toddler in potty training mode, and a husband who was working full time while taking night courses for his holistic nutritional program, who did I turn to when I was crying in despair because I just couldn't handle the stress and overwhelm anymore? My amazing parents, who are always ready and willing to support me. Asking for support is key however not always easy for everyone because people might worry about appearing weak, they may feel ashamed of bothering others, or have difficulty giving up control to someone else.

Support isn't only informal, it can also look like paid work to someone else. I never grew up in a household where we paid someone to help clean our home because it just didn't make any sense to my parents. However I value spending time on things that I want to do and sometimes cleaning my kitchen cabinets isn't how I'd like to spend my time on a Saturday morning when there's an unending list of other important things to do so I outsource the work. I employ someone to do that task for me. I choose to trade in my money for time. Here's another way to spin it - by me having this need for this service, it helps the person being employed to help pay their bills. Once again, I see it as a WIN-WIN. While this may not be possible for everyone, I know it's what works for us and the point here is that you will invest your time and money into the things you truly value.

Support is not always in the receiving but also in the giving. It's important to me to support others but if it means I'm not able to care for my essential needs, then the person I need to support first is myself so that eventually I can help and support others when I'm in the right frame of mind and feeling the balance and harmony in my life.

All this to highlight that "No man is an island" as coined by John Donne - We have to remember that we need each other and in having connections with other people it is essential for our well-being, survival and may I add, for thriving and achieving great things.

-Hybrid-

A friend introduced to me the term "Hybrid" when it comes to parenting and being productive simultaneously. In other words, the meaning of Hybrid is multitasking. So it might look like this - getting my kids involved in helping out with household tasks while I supervise them and do the same or another task nearby. For example, having my 8 yr old son wash his snack and lunch containers while I'm nearby drying and putting away the dishes. Of course there may be an initial investment of time because I need to teach him how to keep the water in the sink and not have it spill all over the floor. But after a few supervised sessions of dish washing, I'm a lot more hands off because I now trust he knows what to do. So not only do household chores get done, my kids start to learn some responsibility in the process. Now that's a WIN-WIN! This isn't always a common occurrence to be truthful because I often want to get things done quickly and I may not have the time or patience to be in teacher mode with my kids. Plus, the ages of my kids as well as their personalities can be factors that can determine how effective this goes. I just think, something is better than nothing and I have to start somewhere. I also have to let go of any expectations of perfection and not lose my cool when my kids don't do something the way I would.

chapter 6 [The Re-Evaluation]

"What is my current inventory and level of satisfaction now?"

After spending time on ourselves and deciding what balance means to us and how we believe is the best way to achieve it, what is our level of satisfaction in the different areas of our life now? Have we found that balance we were looking for? And if not, what areas in our life still feel unbalanced? Where are we still feeling a void?

Well here's the truth. Sometimes there has to be some imbalance for a short while because when we become hard focused on achieving a specific goal, it will consume a lot of our time - time that is already limited to begin with. That is okay knowing that this goal will ultimately lead to the bigger picture of true happiness with us and our family.

Take for example the time when we were parents to our very young and highly dependent children. We were likely less available to our usual social and familial circles (unless they had kids around the same ages) because we were consumed with being the life givers to these little people. I think that warrants taking time away from the usual social obligations or leisurely pleasures we might have otherwise indulged in before having kids.

Something has got to give though – focusing on one thing means that some other part of our life may get overlooked or neglected. We need to choose what we'll be ok with letting go of (in the interim) because the reality is we can't do everything we want at the exact same time but it doesn't mean they still can't get done. They will happen, just at another time. If we even attempt to do every single thing we want to do at the same time, that will only lead to burnout! And by the time we reach this point, we won't be able to do anything at all.

I know when I've become extremely focused on one thing, one of the consequences is my unavailability. You can't find me – I've gone MIA. If I'm not responding to your messages, my intention is not of a disrespectful nature, just know I'm maximizing every second I have towards my goals and other responsibilities. So I need to keep my focus vigilant and strong, otherwise any distraction will interfere with me being in the zone.

We just have to give ourselves the permission and grace to hide away in our corners sometimes but know the cycle is predictable – we will surface again. What we focus on grows so if we have that big goal we need to achieve or those responsibilities we have to fulfill, we have to temporarily put all our eggs in that one basket for now.

-Who Am I When I'm Feeling Balanced and at Peace?-

Imbalance is okay because it's a sign that we need to find a way to become re-aligned with ourselves to have access to that peace and balance we so desire. And after re-evaluating what's not been working and we take action to make those necessary adjustments, all should feel right.

In my world, when all feels right...

I'm a mom who is productive in the house, pays her bills on time and has a clean toilet bowl.

I'm a mom who makes strong connections with my kids and makes memories with them.

I'm a mom who books a massage for herself.

I'm a mom who has a night out for dinner with her girlfriends.

I'm a mom who gets her work done, takes a lunch break, and leaves work on time.

I'm a mom who has a dream goal and works towards it little by little, one step at a time.

I'm a mom who gives hugs and kisses to her kids and doesn't yell...as much.

I'm a mom who can live with dishes piled up in the sink while I help my kid do his homework.

I'm a mom who can be on top of her game but also be ok when things just don't go as planned.

I'm a mom who will roll with the punches and find a solution.

Am I like this everyday? Gosh no! But I have more of these days than I ever have before and I aspire to have more of them.

So how did I get here again?

Let's review some steps:

1. **[Inventory]**: Evaluate the areas of satisfaction and dissatisfaction - How are you feeling in each of the 7 life categories? (Relationships, Career, Physical, Leisure, Home and Living Environment, Spiritual/Personal Development, Finance)
2. **[Goals]**: Improve in the life categories you're already satisfied with. Achieve more or better in the life categories you're dissatisfied with
3. **[Action Steps]**: Take small steps towards the larger goal/bigger picture. *Don't forget to use your powerful mindset and tools to help you along.*
4. **[Re-evaluation and Re-calibration]**: Where might you still feel a void in areas of your life? Put focus on those areas to feel realigned and balanced.

conclusion - [This Is Not The End]

This book isn't about telling you how to live a perfect life because there is no such thing. It's about a life by design, a life that you want to live. Believe it or not, almost everything in your life has not happened by chance, it has happened by choice. Know that there are the conscious choices we make based on emotion, logic, and reason but there are other choices that we make on a subconscious level and those are based on our deep rooted belief systems. I have been on a mission to determine what my subconscious beliefs are and am working on reprogramming them so that I can truly be happy with the life I live. And true happiness for me is when I live in harmony - meaning I have Balance (fulfilling my family's needs alongside my own needs) and peace (living my life with as minimal stress as possible) again contributing ultimately towards my happiness.

Recap of what I've learned:

- Balance means fulfilling my needs, my family's needs while being productive by accomplishing tasks off my list.
- Peace in my life means I don't sweat the small stuff and have control over the stressors in my life. Here I use my tools to help me through any blocks I might encounter

- Despite a busy life I can still have dreams and goals for myself
- By prioritizing and putting my attention and focus on something I'll accomplish anything I set my mind to. This will often require me to ask for support.
- Whenever I'm out of alignment, I will always find a way to adjust and get myself back in a state of balance.

I hope that by this point of the book you start believing in what's possible despite the busy parent-work-family life you may have. Yes, you want to give everything to your family and you want to see them happy, however this is an opportunity to think about how to start putting yourself first. Because when you're good, the people around you are good. By giving to yourself, you are also giving to others.

-"YOU DO YOU!"-

Don't let anyone else's judgments and opinions sway or dictate the way you should be living your life or what that should look like. I'm sure we all can share an experience where the choices we've made in our life weren't really of our own merit or decision. But we live and we learn.

This isn't the end because if we're looking to improve ourselves and our situations, by using tools and processes that are effective for us, we inevitably transform and grow. We just have to choose this path of <u>progress over perfection</u>. I'm so grateful for having been chosen to become a parent because I have learned so much about myself along this journey. What I've learned has extended beyond my role as a parent into other facets of my life. When you're having to raise decent human beings in the midst of a chaotic life, there is no doubt you know what true resilience means. It doesn't mean we don't fall down and scrape our knees - but we do rise up, get back on our feet again and dust ourselves off so we can take another step forward.

-Final Thought: A Poem-

Maybe parenting isn't about achieving perfection but rather of Balance, Peace and Harmony
so that we may be connected with both our children and with ourselves.
That's what I believe true happiness to be.
Why is Balance so important?
Because when we're feeling off-centered,
whether too focused or consumed by either ourselves (the chores, our own thoughts, personal pursuits, vested interests and pleasures)
or our children (their interests, their well-being, their happiness, their upbringing),
when we get pulled too far in either direction
we cannot find happiness at either end
- not truly.
We must find ourselves somewhere in the middle
where our authentic selves are realized and that of our children.
We must be true to ourselves and let our children be true to themselves.
Only when we are true to ourselves can our children be truly free to be who they are meant to be.

-Mayleen Torres-Hew Wing

Hoping there were things you took away from the book, it would be most appreciated if you could leave a favourable review on Amazon. With many blessings and gratitude.

resources

Balance, L. I. T. M.-. (2020, October 18). *10 life areas to set goals to balance it all.* Imperfect Life Balance. Retrieved April 2, 2022, from https://impe rfectlifebalance.com/goal-setting-how-to-plan-and-track-your-go als

Balance, L. I. T. M.-. (2021, September 7). *How to Balance Work and FAMILY in 5 steps – Working Mom Tips.* Imperfect Life Balance. Retrieved April 2, 2022, from https://imperfectlifebalance.com/how-to-balance-it-all-working-mom-tips

E. (2020, November 14). *'No Man Is An Island': Meaning & Context*✔. No Sweat Shakespeare. Retrieved April 2, 2022, from https://nosweatshak espeare.com/quotes/famous/no-man-is-an-island/

Clear, J. (2018). *Atomic Habits: An Easy & Proven Way to Build Good Habits & Break Bad Ones* (Illustrated ed.) [E-book]. Avery.

Ed.D., N. J., Tamborski, M. N., & Ainge, B. (2016). *Positive Discipline Parenting Tools: The 49 Most Effective Methods to Stop Power Struggles, Build Communication, and Raise Empowered, Capable Kids* (Illustrated ed.) [E-book]. Harmony.

Faber, J., & King, J. (2017). *How to Talk so Little Kids Will Listen: A Survival Guide to Life with Children Ages 2–7 (The How To Talk Series)* (Illustrated ed.) [E-book]. Scribner.

INTEGRIS Health. (n.d.). *Why It's Important to Allow Yourself to Rest.* Retrieved April 2, 2022, from https://integrisok.com/resources/on-your-health/2021/april/why-its-important-to-allow-yourself-to-rest

Kurcinka, M. S. (2015). *Raising Your Spirited Child, Third Edition: A Guide for Parents Whose Child Is More Intense, Sensitive, Perceptive, Persistent, and Energetic (Spirited Series)* (3rd ed.) [E-book]. William Morrow Paperbacks.

Lansbury, J. (2014). *No Bad Kids: Toddler Discipline Without Shame* (1st Edition) [E-book]. CreateSpace Independent Publishing Platform.

Muir, N. (2020, May 7). *A Mark's Eye View: Wrestling's most shocking gimmick changes. AIPT. Retrieved April 2, 2022, from* https://aiptcomics.com/2020/05/07/wrestling-gimmick-wwe-bushwhackers/

Proctor, B. (2021). *Change Your Paradigm, Change Your Life* [E-book]. G&D Media.

Quotelia. (n.d.). *Life doesn't happen to you, it happens for you.* Retrieved April 2, 2022, from https://quotelia.com/life-doesnt-happen-to-you

ROBBINS RESEARCHINTERNATIONAL, INC. (2021, December 30). *How to surround yourself with good people in your life.* Tonyrobbins.Com. Retrieved April 2, 2022, from https://www.tonyrobbins.com/stories/business-mastery/surround-yourself-with-quality-people/

Siegel, D. J., & Bryson, T. P. (2012). *The Whole-Brain Child: 12 Revolutionary Strategies to Nurture Your Child's Developing Mind* (Illustrated ed.) [E-book]. Bantam.
49

Siegel, D. J., & Bryson, T. P. (2014). *No-Drama Discipline.* Penguin Random House.

Tseytlovskiy, P. (2019, October 15). *When is lunchtime in a virtual company?* Datapavel. Retrieved April 2, 2022, from https://datapavel.com/blog/when-is-lunchtime-in-a-virtual-company